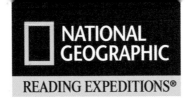

D1649199

KIDS AROUND THE WORLD

Hopes and Dreams

A Story from Northern Thailand

By Jean Bennett
Illustrated by Greg Ruhl

PICTURE CREDITS
3-7, 45-48 (borders) © Roshel Rivellino; 6
Mapping Specialists, Ltd.; 7 (top right) ©
Macduff Everton/Corbis; 7 (center) © Paul
Chesley/Getty Images; 7 (bottom right) © Pete
Turner/Getty Images; 45 © Jan Dago/Getty
Images; 46 (top) © Claver Carroll/Lonely
Planet Images; 46 (bottom) © Larry Dale
Gordon/Getty Images; 48 Courtesy Shingu
Sister City Association, (background) ©
Photodisc/Getty Images.

**PUBLISHED BY THE NATIONAL
GEOGRAPHIC SOCIETY**
Produced through the worldwide resources
of the National Geographic Society, John M.
Fahey, Jr., President and Chief Executive
Officer; Gilbert M. Grosvenor, Chairman of
the Board.

**PREPARED BY NATIONAL GEOGRAPHIC
SCHOOL PUBLISHING**
Sheron Long, Chief Executive Officer; Samuel
Gesumaria, President; Francis Downey, Vice
President and Publisher; Richard Easby,
Editorial Manager; Anne M. Stone, Editor;
Margaret Sidlosky, Director of Design and
Illustrations; Jim Hiscott, Design Manager;
Cynthia Olson, Ruth Ann Thompson, Art
Directors; Matt Wascavage, Director of
Publishing Services; Lisa Pergolizzi,
Production Manager.

MANUFACTURING AND QUALITY CONTROL
Christopher A. Liedel, Chief Financial Officer;
Phillip L. Schlosser, Vice President; Clifton M.
Brown III, Director.

CONSULTANT
Mary Anne Wengel

BOOK DESIGN
Steve Curtis Design, Inc.

Published by the National Geographic Society
1145 17th Street N.W.
Washington, D.C. 20036-4688

Product #4U1005105
ISBN: 978-1-4263-5098-6

Printed in the U.S.A.

15 16 17 18 19 20
10 9 8 7 6 5 4

Contents

Thailand

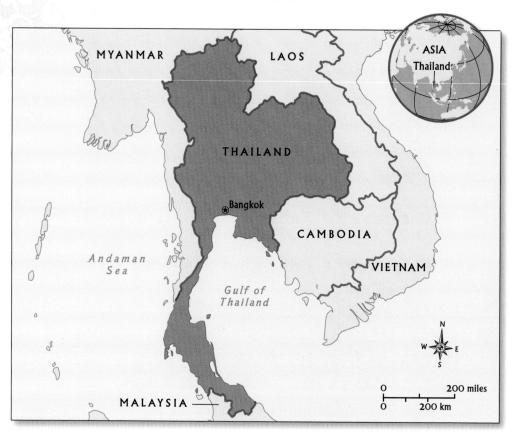

Thailand is a long, narrow country in Southeast Asia. It touches two bodies of water and four countries. Thailand's capital is Bangkok. The country has both a king and elected leaders in its government. The king no longer has much power. But many Thai people still respect him as a symbol of their nation.

Geography

Thailand is about the size of Texas. Northern and central Thailand have rolling hills and valleys. Land there is good for farming. Other parts of Thailand have steep mountains, flat plains, or tropical forests.

Climate

Thailand has different climates depending on the location. Northern and central Thailand have three seasons—a rainy season, a cool season, and a hot season. The rainy season is the longest of the three.

People

More than 60 million people live in Thailand. Most speak the Thai language and practice the Buddhist religion. In the past, most people were farmers. Today, many are leaving their farms to live and work in cities.

Hopes and Dreams

Tal

Tal (pronounced TARN) is a boy living in northern Thailand. He is proud of his traditional culture. He also likes rock music.

Sunan

Sunan (SUH-NUN) is Tal's friend. He wishes that more visitors could see Thai dancing, art, and music.

Tasanee

Tasanee (TUH-SUH-NEE) is Tal's cousin. She learns traditional dances in school and likes performing them.

Mali

Mali (MUH-LEE) is Tal's older sister. She works at a special hospital for elephants. She wants to save the Asian elephants that remain in Thailand.

Tal's Parents

Tal's parents are rice farmers. They like farming, but it is hard work. They want to make a better life for their children.

CHAPTER ONE

Three Friends

Tal woke to the shrill crowing of the family rooster. He saw the first rays of morning light. They streaked through the bamboo matting covering the walls. Tal blinked away the sleep. The rooster crowed again.

"Noisy thing," Tal muttered. "It should be put in a cooking pot."

He pushed the mosquito net away from his thin mattress on the floor. Small lizards darted up the wall as he opened the window shutters. Tal pulled on his school shirt and shorts and went outside. Mist hung over the nearby creek and houses. The air was still. In the distance, Tal heard the village monks chanting their morning prayers.

The door of the small outside washroom was closed. Tal heard his older sister humming inside. The water gurgled as she filled the washbowl. Tal got a mischievous look in his eye. He picked up a speckled frog that was sitting on the brick path. He tiptoed over to the washroom. Silently, he dropped the frog over the gap at the top of the door. Mali shrieked. The door burst open, and she tossed a bowl of water at him.

"Pest!" she yelled, and slammed the door. Tal grinned. He knew she didn't really mind. It was just *sanuk*, good fun.

In the kitchen, Tal's mother was cooking eggs for breakfast. His father was watching the morning weather report. The rainy season had begun. The forecast predicted more heavy rains in the afternoon.

Tal's father sighed. His face was creased with worry. "Rice needs plenty of rain to grow," he said. "But it doesn't need floods." He went outside to put on his boots and check the fields of rice. Each day Tal's parents worked in the fields, or paddies. They inspected the mud banks that surrounded the fields. If the banks failed, the rice plants would be washed away. What would the family do then?

Tal worried about his mother and father. They looked tired from long days bent over rice plants in the paddies. "Isn't there an easier way to earn a living?" he asked his sister.

"Rice farming is all they know," Mali said. "They couldn't afford to go to school. That's why they work so hard to pay for our education. They want us to have more choices." Mali dreamed of being a **veterinarian.** She traveled each morning to the elephant hospital in the forest.

Tal fed the hens and packed his school bag. He took his sandals from the shoe rack by the door. *"Chok dee,"* he said to Mali. "Good luck."

She smiled and put an arm around his neck to give him a hug. Tal felt something slide down his back. He pulled up his shirt. A tiny lizard fell to the floor and shot out of sight.

---

veterinarian – an animal doctor, also called a vet

"Got you!" Mali laughed.

Tal walked down the dusty track toward the main road. On the way, he passed the vast rice fields. His father stood knee-deep in muddy water. A straw hat with a wide brim shaded his face.

"*Sawatdee!* Hello!" Tal heard someone say. It was his cousin Tasanee. She was waiting for him outside her house. Her white blouse and dark blue skirt were freshly ironed. They walked to the corner of the main road and met their classmate Sunan. Together, the three friends walked toward school.

The road was busy at that hour. Many people were headed to the market. An elderly woman pulled her cart of fruits and vegetables along the edge of the road. A scooter loaded with a crate of hens spluttered past. Then a rusty truck rattled into view. Suddenly, a pack of barking dogs ran into the middle of the road. The truck swerved wildly around the dogs—and straight toward the old woman.

"Look out!" Tal shouted. The truck swung back across the road. It just missed the startled woman. The three friends ran to help her. She was shaken but unhurt.

"Mai pen rai. Never mind," she said to the children. "I'm all right." She bent to pick up a few vegetables that had fallen from her cart.

"We're on our way to school," Tal said. "But we can help you get to market first." Tasanee walked ahead with the woman while Tal and Sunan pulled the cart.

Along the way, Tal saw an old elephant standing in a stream. A mahout, the elephant's handler, scrubbed its back. The elephant sucked up water with its trunk, then sprayed it over its back, showering them both.

Tal dug into his pocket and found a few *baht* he'd been saving. He gave the money to the woman and took a bunch of bananas from her cart. Quickly he slid down to the stream. He gave some bananas to the mahout, then held out the rest to the elephant. She plucked the fruit from his hand with her trunk.

"Where are you going today?" Tal asked.

"We've been hired for a wedding," the mahout said. "The guests like to walk under Kanya's belly for good luck."

"Has Kanya ever lived in the forest?" Tal asked.

"She was born there," the mahout answered. "We used to work together in the forest logging trees.

---

baht – a unit of money in Thailand

But then the government **banned** logging. So we had to find other work. Now we spend our days looking for tourists. They pay to have their photos taken with Kanya."

Tal patted Kanya's trunk and said goodbye to the mahout. He climbed back up to the road and told his friends about Kanya.

"It's sad that Kanya has to wander around the villages trying to earn a few *baht*," Tasanee said.

"Elephants should be roaming free in the forest," Sunan agreed.

The three friends continued down the road with the old woman. They waited at the railway crossing while the passenger train to Chiang Mai rattled past. Then they pulled the vegetable cart over the tracks to the market. The children waved goodbye to the woman. They hurried on toward school.

----

ban – to prohibit or make illegal

CHAPTER TWO

Kanya Gets Into Trouble

Tal, Tasanee, and Sunan put their sandals on a shelf. Then they filed into their classroom. They pressed their hands together and bowed to their teacher.

"Good morning," the students greeted her.

"I hope we don't have English lessons," Tasanee whispered. "It's a hard language."

But as soon as they sat down, their teacher said, "Take out your English books, please." Tal heard Tasanee sigh, and grinned. The classmates spent the morning trying to speak to each other in English.

At last, the lunch bell rang. They could speak in Thai again. They filed into the dining hall and waited in line for their food. When it was

Tal's turn, the cook gave him a plate of hot chicken, bamboo shoots, and rice. Tal thanked the cook with a bow. The three friends took their lunch to a table and sat on a bench to eat.

"I've got dance classes this afternoon," Tasanee said.

"We've got music," Sunan said.

"I like Thai music," Tal said. "But I'd rather be a drummer in a famous rock band like on TV."

"In your dreams!" Sunan laughed.

"We spend ages learning Thai music, dancing, and art," Tasanee said. "I wish we could show visitors how beautiful it all is."

"The sword dancers are amazing," Sunan said. "The kickboxing team is too."

"But who sees them?" Tal said. "Hardly anyone ever visits our village."

"There's always lots of tourists on the train to Chiang Mai," Sunan said. "If only they would stop in our village!"

After lunch, the friends went separate ways. Tasanee went to her dance class. Tal and Sunan headed for the music room.

Tal thumped his *glong* drum gently. He
watched Sunan tune the strings on his *zueng.*
The instrument looked a bit like a guitar. Maybe
one day they would be in a rock bank together,
Tal thought.

His daydream dissolved when the music
teacher clapped his hands for attention. Soon
the room was filled with the sound of bamboo
pipes and high-pitched stringed instruments.
Their teacher listened and nodded. "Not bad,"
he said. "Let's try it again."

"Phew!" Tal said to Sunan when the final school bell rang. "That was hard work. I'm glad we're finished for the day."

The three friends collected their bags and sandals for the walk home. Although it was only mid-afternoon, the sky was dark with clouds. "It looks like we'll get soaked," Sunan said.

Soon the rain pelted down. Thunder boomed and lightning flashed in the sky. Water flooded the roadside and flowed over the road. Cars and trucks drove past, drenching the three friends with spray. "I can hardly see where I'm going," Tasanee grumbled.

"We're nearly home," Tal said. Just ahead, he caught sight of the mahout riding Kanya. The elephant plodded slowly along.

Just then, the pack of dogs bounded out of the grass. They barked and snapped at Kanya's legs. The elephant swung her trunk and knocked one dog away. The others continued to hound her. She moved to avoid them, but stepped right into the path of a passing truck. It blasted its horn at Kanya. She trumpeted in terror.

"Oh no!" Tal cried. He saw Kanya shake her head and toss the mahout from her neck.

The frightened elephant lumbered into a sugarcane field. Plants crumpled under her big feet. The mahout ran after her, shouting commands as he went.

"We've got to help!" Tal said. Sunan and Tasanee followed him into the field. They stumbled over the flattened plants and caught

up with the mahout in a corner of the field. Kanya stood in front of them. She tore at the sugarcane with her trunk and bundled it into her mouth.

Tal heard angry shouts. He looked around. The farmer and his family were coming toward them. They waved long sticks. "Get out!" the farmer yelled. "Get that beast out of my field!"

Startled, Kanya turned to escape. She lurched sideways. One foot sank into a ditch. Her huge body thumped to the ground. She tried to rise, but fell back again. She lay there in the field. Her sides were heaving.

"She's hurt her leg," the mahout called.

"What can we do?" Sunan said.

"Mali will know," Tal said. "Tasanee, run home and call the elephant hospital. We'll stay here with the mahout."

Within an hour, a rescue team from the elephant hospital arrived. Mali was among the white-coated veterinarians. Tal watched as she helped the rescue team calm the frightened, injured elephant.

A veterinarian gave Kanya medicine to numb her pain. Then the team used a tow truck to help winch her out of the ditch. They put a harness, or sling, under her. A crane lifted her onto the back of another truck. It would take her to the elephant hospital.

Mali patted Tal's shoulder. "You did well," she said. She gave him a smile.

"And you'll be a great vet," Tal said. But still, he couldn't help feeling worried. What would happen to the elephant and her mahout?

CHAPTER THREE

Floods in the Fields

In the coming days, rainstorms flooded the land. Strong winds tore at trees and crops.

At times the sun shone briefly. But dark clouds always rolled back across the sky. One day when Tal came home from school, his father sat at the table with his head in his hands.

"The floods have weakened the mud banks in the rice paddies," he said. "I've strengthened the banks. But if they collapse, the rice plants will wash away."

"Each year you work too hard and worry too much," Tal said. "There must be a better way."

His mother agreed. "Rice farmers are supposed to be the backbone of Thailand," she said. "But this work is breaking our backs."

Tal's father sighed. "Perhaps I should go to Chiang Mai and look for a job," he said.

"You're not going to work in that crowded, noisy city," Tal's mother said. "It's too far away. We'd have to leave the village. Besides, the wages are poor. We'll manage somehow."

But Tal knew that if the rice crop failed, they wouldn't have enough money to survive. They would be forced to leave the village and find work in the city.

Stormy weather returned with gale-force winds. Driving rain stung Tal's face as he walked to and from school. Each day, Tal's father waded through deep water in the rice paddies. He

patched gaps in the mud banks only to have new ones appear the next day. More and more plants were washed away.

Late one afternoon, Tal's mother looked outside. "Your father isn't home yet," she said in a worried voice.

"He's probably on his way," Tal said. "I'll go meet him." He walked toward the paddies, but there was no sign of his father. He looked across at the swamped rice plants. Rain blurred his vision. "Father!" he shouted. "Where are you?"

There was no reply. Tal waded between the plants. "Father! Can you hear me?" he called again and again.

At last, a faint voice replied. "Over here!" Tal stumbled toward the sound. He found his father slumped over a mud bank. "My ankle," his father groaned. "I've twisted it."

"Hold on to me," Tal said. His father put his arm around Tal's shoulders. Tal helped him up. They slowly made their way out of the rice paddy. Tal half-carried his father along the road. His mother ran to meet them and helped them the rest of the way home.

"You must rest," Tal's mother said. She wound a firm bandage around her husband's ankle. He nodded, lay back on the bed, and closed his eyes.

After school each day, Tal went to the rice fields and strengthened the mud banks. The rains eased and the banks held.

"A lot of plants have survived," he told his father one evening.

"You're a good son," he answered. "I worry that the rice crop won't earn enough for you to have a good education. I want you to have a better life than a rice farmer."

"What is more important," Tal said, "is that you don't ever have to leave your village and home. And that you don't have to work this hard."

Tal went outside and stood by the creek. He watched crabs scuttle around the banks. He heard a dog howl in the distance. Wind rustled the leaves of the palm trees.

Tal loved village life, his family, and his friends. But he wondered what the future held for them. Sometimes he dreamed about living in a big city. Maybe one day he'd win a music **scholarship** and travel overseas! What would his father think then? Was that what he meant by a better life? Tal sighed. He wasn't sure.

scholarship – money given to someone to help pay for education

CHAPTER FOUR

Surprise Visitors

One night Mali came home from the elephant hospital smiling. "Our elephant friend is doing well," she said. "Kanya's leg has nearly healed."

"Great!" Tal said. Then he frowned. "But what will happen to her when she leaves the elephant hospital?"

Mali's smile faded. "I'm not sure," she said. "There's a big forest reserve near the hospital. A few elephants and their mahouts live there. They've set up a center to show tourists the old logging skills. They also take visitors for rides in the forest."

"It sounds perfect for Kanya," Tal said. "What's the problem?"

"Not many people visit the center," Mali explained. "So they don't have enough money to keep it going—or to let new elephants and mahouts join them."

"There's never enough money!" Tal groaned. "What are we going to do?"

The next day on the way to school, Tal told Tasanee and Sunan about Kanya's problem.

"We can't just let her go back to wandering the streets," Tasanee said. "She needs to be free in the forest."

They came to the railway crossing. They waited behind a cart pulled by two cows. A young man with a stick prodded the animals to cross the tracks. The cows were halfway across when Tal noticed the back wheel of the cart wobble. Before he could shout a warning, the axle broke with a crack. The cart toppled over. Both animals were dragged to their knees.

A whistle sounded down the line. "A train's coming!" Tasanee cried. The friends ran to help the young man unharness the cows. One animal scrambled up. Tasanee led it away from the tracks. But the other cow struggled to stand.

"Get back!" shouted Tal. "We can't save it."
He pulled Sunan away as the train rattled
toward them. The train's brakes screeched.
Sparks sprayed out from its wheels as it tried to
stop. At the last second, the cow scrambled up
and off the tracks to safety. The next moment,
the engine hit the cart and splintered it into

pieces. The passenger cars shuddered. One twisted sideways across the tracks. Frightened cries came from the train. People clambered out of the cars in a daze. Tal, Tasanee, and Sunan ran to help. Villagers and monks came to take care of the shaken travelers.

"There doesn't seem to be anyone badly hurt," Tasanee said. "Just a few cuts and some bruises."

"It will be ages before the track is cleared and the train can run again," Sunan said.

Rain began to fall. A number of tourists huddled around their Thai leader. Tal saw American and Canadian flags stuck to a few of their backpacks.

"We have to look after them," Tasanee said. She went over to the leader of the group. "You need shelter," she said. "Please come with us. Our school is just down the road."

"*Kawp khun ka.* Thank you," the leader said. "It will be good to go somewhere dry."

The school principal greeted the visitors warmly. "Our school is your home for today," he said. He turned to Tal, Tasanee, and Sunan. "I'm pleased you've shown Thai hospitality to our guests. You can be their school guides while they are with us."

"Please, may I make a suggestion?" Tal asked. The principal nodded. Tal said, "We should show our visitors about Thai culture and music."

"That's a good idea. Run and tell the teachers to prepare for guests."

Soon the school was alive with activity. The three friends took the visitors on a tour of the school. They stopped by the arts room with its colorful displays of traditional crafts. Classes buzzed with students trying to speak English with the guests.

In the dining halls, the school cooks prepared lunch for the extra people. Villagers arrived with bowls of rice, fried chicken, and stir-fried vegetables to help feed the guests. They had never seen so many visitors in their town!

After lunch, everyone gathered in the school hall for a special performance. The orchestra played Thai music. A group of girls danced the traditional *fawn leb* dance. They were dressed in silk. Their long, golden fingernails shone. Next, several boys ran onto the floor. They wore blue shirts and pants. They had red scarves tied around their heads. Tal pounded out a beat. The boys leaped into action and twirled their swords. Then the school's Thai kickboxing team took center stage.

At the end of the performance, the visitors stood and clapped loudly. As the students

packed away their concert gear, the leader of the tour group found Tal, Tasanee, and Sunan.

"Your hospitality today has been wonderful," he said. "And the concert was superb. I hope this is the start of many visits I make to your school and village."

"What do you mean?" asked Tal.

"I run a tourist business," he explained. "I've been looking for a village where I can set up farm tours, traditional craft displays, school visits, and cultural performances."

Tal looked thoughtful. "Would you like to include tours to an elephant center in the forest?" he asked.

"Visitors would love that," the tour guide said. Tal smiled. Maybe the old ways of life could survive after all!

That night, almost every house in the village had guests. Tal's parents gave their room to two men working for the Thai government. The visitors talked long into the night with Tal's parents. Tal fell asleep to the sound of their voices.

Several times in the following weeks, Tal came home from school to find strangers talking with his parents. One day he watched his father take the visitors to the paddy fields.

"What's going on?" he asked his mother.

"Do you remember the men who stayed here the night of the train accident?" she asked. Tal nodded. "One of them knew about a plan to help struggling rice farmers," his mother said. "The government wants farmers to try new crops. It will even help with set-up costs."

"Why do you want carry on with farm work?" Tal asked. "Isn't the tourist business a better way to earn money?"

Tal's mother patted his shoulder. "I know you want us to have an easier life," she said. "Tourism will help many of the villagers, in time. But your father and I have always been farmers. It's what we know. We're happy if we can earn enough from the land to provide for our family."

In the coming weeks, the rainy season passed. The sky brightened, and crops ripened in the fields.

"We'll harvest enough rice to cover our debts," Tal's father reported one evening. "Then we'll clear the fields and build huts for our new mushroom farm. It will be an easier crop for us to manage."

"It will be good to work under shelter," Tal's mother said. "Mushrooms grow all year round so we'll have a regular income."

"I'm glad you're happy," Tal said. "Now we can really celebrate the Loy Krathong festival tomorrow!"

CHAPTER FIVE

Big Plans

The next day, the school grounds swarmed with people. They were all preparing for a parade. People decorated trucks in flowers and bright ribbons. They set up huge models of dragons, tigers, and elephants on the trucks. In the late afternoon, the school orchestra climbed into the back of a truck.

"We get to lead the parade," Sunan said.

"And I get to play the biggest *glong!*" Tal said.

Tasanee walked past, holding up her long skirt to keep the hem clean. "See you by the river," she called.

Students lined up behind the trucks. Some held bowl-shaped *krathong* flower arrangements with candles and incense sticks. Others carried colored paper lanterns. "Here we go," Tal said. He pounded on the drums.

The trucks rolled slowly onto the road to the river. Other trucks from the village joined the parade. Many people stood along the road. They watched as the parade passed. Tal saw the tour leader who had visited their school. He was with a group of eager visitors taking photos.

Tal glanced up as they came to a crossroads.

"Look!" he said to Sunan. Kanya the elephant plodded toward them. The mahout rode on her neck. A brightly painted *howdah* seat was tied to the elephant's back.

"Kanya's leg has healed well," Sunan said, watching the elephant's steady walk.

A young woman dressed in a Thai costume
sat in the *howdah*. "It's Mali!" Tal said. Kanya
raised her trunk in greeting, and Mali waved.

Late in the day, villagers crowded along the
riverbank. People lit the candles and incense
sticks on their *krathongs*. They placed their
flower arrangements in the water. They gave
thanks to the river. The full moon rose higher.
Firecrackers sparked and exploded into the
night sky.

Tal held up a *khom loy* paper lantern. Sunan
tied a kerosene-soaked cloth beneath it. Tasanee
lit a match and touched it against the cloth.

It flared up. The three friends held on to the lantern while it filled with smoke.

Tal thought about all the hard work and worries of the past months. Then he let the thoughts leave his mind, just like the smoke rising into the lantern. The *khom loy* took away any bad memories. It shone light on better times to come.

Tasanee said, "Remember to think about your hopes for the future."

Tal hoped that one day he'd travel to other countries and learn new skills. The three friends released the burning lantern. It floated upward to join other flaming *khom loy*.

They watched their lantern float higher and higher. It rose into the night sky, lighting the way for their hopes and dreams. Whatever the future held for him, Tal knew one thing for sure. He'd always come home to Thailand.

Thai Culture

Tal and his family are fictional characters. That means they are made up. But many things about the story are true. Rice is one of Thailand's most important crops. Loy Krathong is a real festival. The street elephants are real too.

Rice Farming

Rice is Thailand's most important crop. It grows on more than half of the country's farmland. Growing rice is hard work. Rice is also a risky crop for farmers. Too much rain, or too little, can ruin the harvest. Farmers plant rice in April and May. They gather it in November or December.

Loy Krathong

Loy Krathong is a festival in November. It honors the goddess of water. People make flower decorations or small boats of banana leaves to float on the river. They also light paper lanterns called *khom loy.* People believe that bad luck floats away with the lanterns—and good fortune comes.

Elephants

Thailand had about 100,000 elephants a century ago. Some of these elephants were trained to plow fields or log timber. The rest lived free. Today, only about 6,000 elephants are left. Half are tame and work in tourism. Most of the rest live in conservation centers. Few elephants roam wild in Thailand today.

Create a Travel Brochure

You read about a plan to bring visitors to northern Thailand. Now help tourists learn about the region. Create a brochure that tells what people can see and do on their travels.

- Research at the library or online. Find out about festivals, food, and fun things to do.

- Decide what to show in your brochure. What is special about this part of Thailand?

- Give each column a heading, such as "For Kids" or "What to See." Write a paragraph for each.

- Search for pictures of Thailand, or draw your own.

- Put your text and pictures together to make a brochure. Use the model below as an example.

For Kids	Festivals	What to See

Food

Read More About Other Cultures

Find and read more books about countries in Asia. As you read, think about these questions. They will help you understand more about this topic.

- What is life like in this country?
- What is special about this country?
- How is this country changing?
- What are people doing to keep their traditions alive?

SUGGESTED READING
Reading Expeditions
Communities Around the World: Shingu, Japan

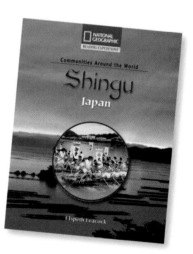

NATIONAL GEOGRAPHIC
READING EXPEDITIONS

Communities Around the World

Shingu
Japan

Elspeth Leacock